SEASONS OF THE YEAR

Winter

by Rebecca Pettiford

BLASTOFF! READERS

BELLWETHER MEDIA • MINNEAPOLIS, MN

Note to Librarians, Teachers, and Parents:

Blastoff! Readers are carefully developed by literacy experts and combine standards-based content with developmentally appropriate text.

Level 1 provides the most support through repetition of high-frequency words, light text, predictable sentence patterns, and strong visual support.

Level 2 offers early readers a bit more challenge through varied simple sentences, increased text load, and less repetition of high-frequency words.

Level 3 advances early-fluent readers toward fluency through increased text and concept load, less reliance on visuals, longer sentences, and more literary language.

Level 4 builds reading stamina by providing more text per page, increased use of punctuation, greater variation in sentence patterns, and increasingly challenging vocabulary.

Level 5 encourages children to move from "learning to read" to "reading to learn" by providing even more text, varied writing styles, and less familiar topics.

Whichever book is right for your reader, Blastoff! Readers are the perfect books to build confidence and encourage a love of reading that will last a lifetime!

This edition first published in 2018 by Bellwether Media, Inc.

No part of this publication may be reproduced in whole or in part without written permission of the publisher. For information regarding permission, write to Bellwether Media, Inc., Attention: Permissions Department, 5357 Penn Avenue South, Minneapolis, MN 55419.

Library of Congress Cataloging-in-Publication Data

Names: Pettiford, Rebecca, author.
Title: Winter / by Rebecca Pettiford.
Description: Minneapolis, MN : Bellwether Media, 2018. | Series: Blastoff! Readers: Seasons of the Year | Includes bibliographical references and index. | Audience: K-3.
Identifiers: LCCN 2017029526 | ISBN 9781626177635 (hardcover : alk. paper) | ISBN 9781681034683 (ebook) | ISBN 9781618913043 (pbk. : alk. paper)
Subjects: LCSH: Winter–Juvenile literature.
Classification: LCC QB637.8 .P48 2018 | DDC 508.2–dc23
LC record available at https://lccn.loc.gov/2017029526

Editor: Christina Leaf   Designer: Josh Brink

Printed in the United States of America, North Mankato, MN.

Table of Contents

Snow and Ice

A heavy snow falls and blankets the trees. Ice cracks under boots.

The smell of chimney smoke fills the frosty air. This is winter!

When Is Winter?

Winter begins after fall. In the **Northern Hemisphere,** winter starts in December.

It lasts through January
and February.

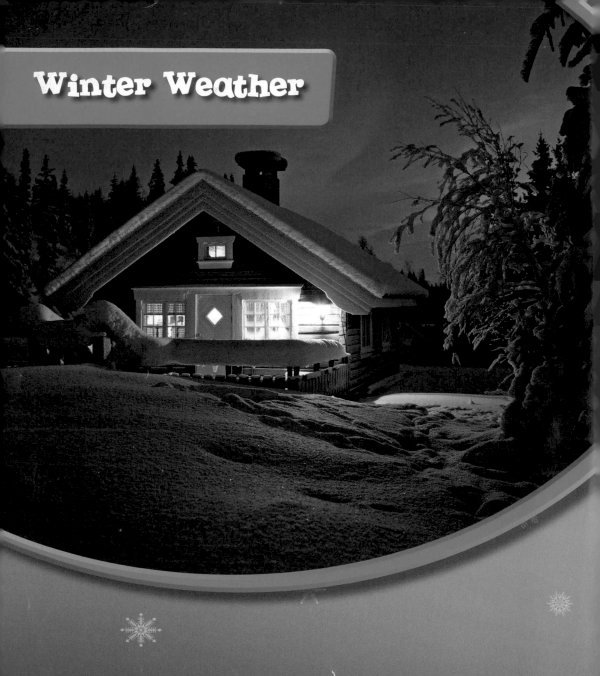

Winter Weather

Winter days are short because Earth's **tilt** allows less sunlight. They are the coldest of the year.

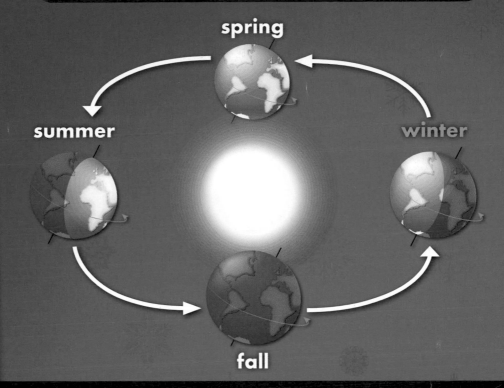

Earth's Position in Winter

spring

summer

winter

fall

Seasons change with the amount of sunlight reaching Earth. The Northern Hemisphere is tilted away from the sun in winter, so it receives less sunlight.

Storms can bring snow, **sleet**, and freezing rain.

Blizzards may shut down schools and businesses. They can drop a lot of snow.

Blizzard Alley

**Blizzard Season:
October to May**

Blizzard Risk

highest risk	high risk	medium risk

Their high winds cause **whiteouts** and **snowdrifts**.

Plants and Animals in Winter

Trees and plants are **dormant** in winter. They stop growing.

Some trees drop their leaves to save water. **Evergreen** leaves can hold in water. They stay on year-round.

evergreen trees

whooper swans migrating

Some animals **migrate** south where it is warmer.

Other animals **hibernate** in dens to save energy. Their heart rates slow and their body **temperatures** drop.

groundhog

Many animals stay active. Some hunt while others eat bark or dig for stored food.

red fox

field mouse

Smaller animals live beneath the snow. Spaces in the snow trap heat.

Thick fur keeps animals warm. Some animals have fur that turns white.

red squirrel

snowshoe hare

It blends with the snow so **predators** cannot see them!

People wear coats, gloves, and hats. They shovel snow and build snow people.

20

They sled, skate, and ski. Inside,
they warm up with hot cocoa!

Glossary

blizzards—powerful storms of blowing snow that last a long time

dormant—not active but able to become active at another time

evergreen—related to trees and plants that stay green all year

hibernate—to spend the winter sleeping or resting

migrate—to move from one place to another, often with the seasons

Northern Hemisphere—the half of the globe that lies north of the equator; the equator is an imaginary line around Earth.

predators—animals that hunt other animals for food

sleet—frozen or partly frozen rain

snowdrifts—hills of snow made by strong winds

temperatures—measurements that indicate how cold or hot things are

tilt—slant or tip

whiteouts—snowstorms in which blowing or falling snow make it hard to see

To Learn More

AT THE LIBRARY

Meister, Cari. *Blizzards*. Mankato, Minn.: Pogo Books, 2016.

Owen, Ruth. *How Do You Know It's Winter?* New York, N.Y.: Bearport Publishing, 2017.

Pak, Kenard. *Goodbye Autumn, Hello Winter*. New York, N.Y.: Henry Holt and Company, 2017.

ON THE WEB
Learning more about winter is as easy as 1, 2, 3.

1. Go to www.factsurfer.com.

2. Enter "winter" into the search box.

3. Click the "Surf" button and you will see a list of related web sites.

With factsurfer.com, finding more information is just a click away.

Index

The images in this book are reproduced through the courtesy of: KellyNelson, front cover; tomch, p. 4; AarreRinne, p. 5; Inu, p. 6; ElenaBelozorova, p. 7; SiriGronskar, p. 8; Designua, p. 9; DenisTangneyJr, p. 10; Thomas Schwarz Fotografie, p. 12; Jorge Moro, p. 13; Grigorii Pisotsckii, p. 14; Brian E Kushner, p. 15; FotoRequest, pp. 16, 19; Sergei Brik, p. 17; ERainbow, p. 18; Dmitry Kalinovsky, p. 21.